Beyond the Grave: A Son's Journey Through Xhosa Tradition, Spirituality, and Freedom

The Harmony of Tradition, Science, and Spirituality in Xhosa Culture

By Salatiso

For Sazi

Copyright

© 2024 Salatiso Lonwabo Mdeni.
All rights reserved.
This book or any portion thereof may not be reproduced or used in any manner whatsoever without the express written permission of the publisher except for the use of brief quotations in a book review.
salatiso@salatiso.com

Dedication

To & for Mlandeli & Sazi,
Solo and all my nephews and nieces,
My mother, and my family—immediate and extended, past, present,
and future.
Tee, without you I may never have returned.

iSazisi

Preface

In my journey of self-discovery, I recently published a book titled "Getting to Know Yourself as a South African: Unravelling Xhosa History: A Journey from Central Africa to South Africa." This work traces the history of the Xhosa people, predominantly found in the former Transkei, now Eastern Cape province of South Africa. Initially, this endeavour was for my own benefit, as I sought to understand more about myself and, subsequently, the diverse peoples of South Africa and the world to find my place within this tapestry. One of the most fascinating revelations was the extensive migration of the Xhosa people, with distant roots in central Africa, ultimately leading to their settlement in the Eastern Cape. This migration meant that many of my ancestors died along the way, leaving their remains scattered and often unburied.

Throughout my life, I have been deeply immersed in the traditions of the Xhosa people, particularly the veneration of ancestors. This reference is not solely out of choice but also because of my life circumstances and my position as the firstborn male in my family. When my father died when I was 11, it became my duty to succeed him. In succeeding him, I knew that the same obligations that applied to me would apply to my son. These burdens shaped my life, and I resolved to shield my son from such weight.

This book is born from that determination. It is primarily written for my son, nephews, and nieces, to provide them with the understanding I struggled to achieve, so they won't have to carry the same burdens I did. My goal is to free them from the physical and emotional constraints that restrained me, allowing them to be whatever they want to be, wherever in the world they may find themselves.

One of the most fascinating revelations in my research was the extensive migration of the Xhosa people, with distant roots in central Africa, ultimately leading to their settlement in the Eastern Cape. This migration meant that many of our ancestors died along the way, leaving their remains scattered and often unburied. This historical context led me to question whether we should honour only those ancestors whose graves we know, especially considering the prospective future for my descendants in today's globalised world.

As I delved deeper into our traditions and history, I encountered practices that seemed at odds with our migratory past and uncertain future. For instance, I learned that in olden times, common people's corpses were often left to be devoured by beasts of prey, while only chiefs and great men were interred with ceremony. This raised questions about where our people historically connected with their ancestors and Qamata (God), especially when graves were unknown or inaccessible due to migrations and conflicts.

These revelations led me to ponder whether the physical disconnection from an ancestor's remains severed our spiritual connection with Qamata. I began to look inward, rather than outward, for a connection with my ancestors. I realised that wherever I am, I embody my ancestors within me. Their physical influence and wisdom are carried in my genes, and my spirit is a continuation of theirs.

This book explores this introspective journey, shedding light on the spiritual omnipresence of ancestors and the broader understanding of our connection to Qamata, integrating Xhosa tradition with scientific and biological perspectives. Through this synthesis, I hope to demonstrate the consistency and harmony between our ancestral reverence and our biological heritage, while also addressing the practical and emotional burdens that traditional practices can place on individuals and families. By sharing my personal experiences and reflections, I aim to offer guidance and solace to others navigating the complexities of cultural identity, ancestral veneration, and the quest for spiritual freedom in the modern world.

Moreover, this work is a testament to my wish for my own remains after I die. I don't want to be a burden to my son or tie him down to a physical location. I prefer for my remains to return to nature, leaving no trace of a monument. If I am to be buried, I want it done simply, without fuss or financial burden on my family.

It is my sincere hope that this book will serve as a guide for future generations, helping them navigate the complex interplay between tradition and modernity. By sharing my journey of questioning, understanding, and ultimately finding peace, I aim to provide a framework for others to honour their heritage while embracing the freedom to forge their own paths in an ever-changing world.

Ultimately, this book is a tribute to my father and a message to my son.

1. A Son's Inheritance: The Weight of Tradition and Responsibility

I was eleven years old when my father died, thrusting me into a role I was far from ready to assume. As the firstborn and only son, I knew that one day I would succeed my father—it was what my culture and tradition demanded. But I never expected that day to come so soon.

Our home in the Eastern Cape, nestled in the heart of Xhosa territory, became a place of mixed emotions. It was where I had my happiest childhood memories, but also where I watched my father's life ebb away. The walls that once echoed with his laughter now stood as silent reminders of the duty I had inherited.

1.1. A Family's Journey

My parents' story was one of progress and determination. From a rental in rural villages like KwaSongwevu, to Mahasana, and ultimately to owning our own home in Drayini, they worked tirelessly to provide for our family. Each move—from Mahasana to Newtown, and finally to Drayini—marked an upward step in our family's journey.

But just as we seemed to be reaching new heights, tragedy struck. My father died in the very home he had built for us, leaving behind a legacy of both achievement and unfulfilled potential.

1.2. The Burden of Expectation

My family—my mother and three sisters—looked to me as the new head of our household. This expectation was further complicated by the traditional roles my parents had assumed. As I grappled with my new responsibilities, I couldn't help but feel a mixture of anger and frustration. I had hoped my father would prepare me for this role, but his work had kept him away from home for long stretches of time.

1.3. Ancestral Bonds: The Xhosa Worldview

To understand the weight of my inheritance, one must grasp the deep-rooted significance of ancestors in Xhosa culture. For us, death is not an end but a transition. Our ancestors are ever-present, guiding us, protecting us, and at times, chastising us when we stray from our path.

1.4. A Clash of Worlds and a Journey of Discovery

However, this traditional worldview increasingly clashes with modern influences. Christianity, Western education, and urban migration have complicated our relationship with these age-old beliefs. As a young man straddling these two worlds, I found myself questioning, reevaluating, and ultimately reimagining my cultural inheritance.

The tragedy of my father's untimely death became the catalyst for my in-depth investigation into my culture and Christianity. I was determined to understand and document these aspects of my life, not just for myself, but for my future son. I wanted to ensure that even if I were to die young, he would have a starting point in understanding his role and heritage.

1.5. The Intersection of Tradition and Modernity

My father's approach to Christianity offered another perspective on bridging tradition and modernity. He was more serious about church than my mother, even taking on responsibilities in the Wesley Methodist Church. What I came to appreciate about Christianity, even when I didn't believe in it for myself, was its emphasis on written records.

Unlike the oral traditions of my people, Christianity offered tangible records that one could read and interpret for oneself. This appreciation for written knowledge was reflected in my parents' insistence on always providing us with books and access to education.

1.6. The Wisdom in Oral Tradition

It would take me almost four decades to understand the ingenuity of not writing but rather passing knowledge orally. Our ancestors seemed to understand the rapid pace of change in the world and didn't want future generations to be bound by outdated practices simply because they were written down.

1.7. The Core of Xhosa Tradition

I came to realise that the central message of Xhosa tradition and spirituality revolves around respect for one's family as the gateway to connecting with our god. This respect extends to both living and deceased. However, I began to question the common interpretation that this respect necessitated an attachment to physical remains and monuments.

1.8. Contextual Rather Than Literal

As I observed the variations in traditional practices across the Eastern Cape, I realised that Xhosa tradition was contextual rather than literal. Practices varied based on geography, available resources, and other local factors. This realisation allowed me to approach our traditions with a critical eye, questioning and interpreting cultural practices to determine their relevance—a skill my father had nurtured in me.

1.9. The Central Dilemma: Honouring the Past, Embracing the Future

At the heart of my story lies a question that has haunted me since childhood: What should I do with my father's remains? This wasn't merely a logistical problem; it was a profound spiritual and cultural dilemma that touched the very core of my identity as a Xhosa man.

As I embarked on this journey of questioning and discovery, I didn't realise that in seeking to lay my father's remains to rest, I would ultimately find a new understanding of life, death, and the enduring connections that bind us all. More importantly, I would find a way to honour my heritage while forging a path that would allow my own son the freedom to navigate his world without the burdensome yoke I had inherited.

1.10. The Power of a Name

My journey of understanding began with my name. While my grandfather had named my father Mlandeli, meaning "to follow," my father chose a different path for me. He named me Salatiso, which roughly translates to "show us the way." This name, dreamt by my father before my birth, carried with it the weight of expectation and the freedom to pioneer. Unlike my father, who had the courage to change my trajectory from that given to him by his father, I found no reason to deviate from his aspirations for me with my son. This is why Sazisi is synonymous with Salatiso, hence I use it in place of contents in my publications.

I have great respect for my grandfather, who named my father Mlandeli. He did what he thought was best for the time, and I'm grateful for his wisdom. Perhaps had my father been given a more challenging name, he might not have lived long enough to have me. I admire my grandfather for playing it safe when it was necessary.

However, I have even more respect for my father who, where it mattered most, didn't conform and follow after his father by cautioning me to play it safe. This took immense courage and foresight. It reflected that in the path given to him by my grandfather, my father learned and chose for me to challenge convention, question it, think critically, and find a way based on logic and reason instead of blind conformance.

In naming my son Sazisi, I am the one who followed my father and extended his aspirations to another generation. These aspirations are even more relevant now, and it's as if my father foresaw this. For the longest time, I was angry at my father for dying and leaving us with limited means, which I deemed as shortcomings. It wasn't until I realised that if I measured my father's progress relative to his father, it became evident how much the man had progressed, which is the most relevant measure of success.

One of the reasons I'm cautious of formal schooling is that rather than teach me to look at my parents' progress, and indeed my grandfather who did better than his father, formal schooling made it seem as if my father had failed because he hadn't achieved certain material means. It was when I looked at my father and grandfather relative to each other that I appreciated the vast effort and success that came with each successive generation.

Until I had a name for my son, I could never have him, which explains why it took me 35 years to have my son, about 10 years later than my father. What took me 35 years to figure out, my father did in 25. Considering that I'm supposed to be smarter than him since I am significantly more educated, this reflects how shortsighted attaching so much to formal knowledge as a measure of wisdom can be.

I came to understand that my grandfather's choice of name for my father was likely influenced by the turbulent times he lived in—a country grappling with the collision of traditional Xhosa beliefs and Western values brought by colonisation. The apartheid laws that impacted the Xhosa people likely made my grandfather cautious, urging my father to play it safe and not question authority.

But my father had different aspirations for me. He wanted me to question the norm, lead rather than follow. This ethos was exemplified in a memory from when I was about six years old. After receiving my report card, my father praised my top ranking but then delved into a detailed discussion about the class averages. He taught me never to measure myself against the norm but to always strive for my best performance.

This continuity of fathers passing their aspirations through their sons, from my grandfather down to the name I gave Sazi, reflects a journey of growth, courage, and wisdom across generations. Each father did what he believed was best for his time, and each successive generation built upon the lessons and progress of the one before.

2. The Weight of Tradition

In Xhosa culture, ancestral veneration is not merely a personal choice—it's a societal imperative. As I grew older, I became acutely aware of my community's watchful eyes and whispered judgments. Ironically, these pressures never came from my immediate family. My mother understood the burden of being a provider, a role I had assumed since I was 20. She appreciated my prioritisation of caring for her and my sisters, who were alive and had tangible needs—just as my father had done during his lifetime.

Neighbours and extended family members began voicing their opinions, sometimes directly, often indirectly. "When will you perform the ritual for your father?" they would ask, their tone a mixture of curiosity and expectation. Some were bolder, suggesting that my success in life—my education, my career—was directly linked to my father's spiritual satisfaction.

The pressure was relentless and multifaceted. There was financial strain from providing for my mother and sisters while building my own life. Rituals and ceremonies were expensive, requiring livestock sacrifices and hosting numerous guests. The outstanding ritual—bringing my father's spirit back home—was particularly demanding. It required slaughtering a cow and other livestock to entertain and feed family members, some travelling from afar to celebrate and make appeals to the spirits, ultimately to Qamata.

Emotional pressure came from the implication that I was neglecting my father's spirit, failing in my duties as a son. Cultural pressure stemmed from the fear that not adhering strictly to these traditions somehow made me less Xhosa, less connected to my roots.

Despite my mother's understanding and my father's teachings, I can't pretend this pressure didn't affect me. It created a constant undercurrent of anxiety in my life. Every achievement was tempered by nagging guilt, every setback interpreted as possible ancestral displeasure. It was a weight

I carried silently, unsure how to reconcile these expectations with my evolving worldview and the practical realities of my life.

2.1. Childhood memories and early understanding

My earliest memories of my father are a mixture of love, admiration, and a child's incomprehension of mortality. I remember his strong hands guiding mine as he taught me woodworking, his deep voice recounting ancestral stories by the fireside, and even the sting of the sjambok when I carelessly left tools outside. These fragmented, fleeting memories became precious anchors to a time before tradition's weight fell upon my shoulders.

As a child, I understood death simply—someone was here, then they were not. The complex spirituality surrounding death in our culture was beyond my grasp. I watched, wide-eyed and confused, as adults performed rituals I didn't understand, speaking to spirits I couldn't see.

One memory stands out vividly: my father's funeral. The solemn atmosphere, the gathering of unfamiliar people, the haunting traditional songs—it all seemed surreal. It was perhaps the first time I'd seen my mother at her weakest, a vulnerability she never displayed even during my father's illness. I watched a cow being slaughtered, its life given to accompany my father on his journey. At eleven years old, I couldn't fully comprehend the significance, but I sensed the gravity of the moment. It was my first real encounter with the intricate dance between life, death, and spiritual belief in our culture.

2.2. Coming of age and assuming responsibilities

As I entered my teens, the abstract concept of 'succeeding my father' began to take concrete form. As the only male in the house, some traditional practices demanded my involvement, even as a teenager, albeit with help from my mother and uncles.

With each passing year, the responsibilities grew. I juggled school demands with my mother's financial constraints, living off my father's pension, which had to support us all. The expectations of being the family's spiritual leader weighed heavily. I had to learn quickly; while urban areas might allow escape from tradition's hold, in our rural village, shared traditions meant strict enforcement, even if only through gossip about unacceptable conduct.

This period was marked by a profound sense of inadequacy. How could I, still a boy in many ways, fill the shoes of a man I was still grieving? Nights found me awake, overwhelmed by expectations, yearning for guidance from the very person whose absence had thrust me into this role.

Yet, slowly, I began to grow into these responsibilities. Each small decision, each ritual performed, each family crisis navigated, added to my confidence. I was becoming the man my father had hoped I would be, even as I grappled with what that truly meant.

2.3. Performing the initial rituals

All necessary rituals but one had been performed after my father's death. The final ritual came when I was in my early 30s, finally able to say his wife and daughters were stable enough, and I could afford the necessary sacrifices. Until then, I reasoned that had he been alive, he would have prioritised the living over the dead, so I prioritised his children and wife before his remains.

The preparation was exciting and terrifying. I consulted with elders, ensuring every detail was correct. The weight of getting it right—for my father, for my family, for my community—was immense.

On the ritual day, I stood before the gathered family, a sharp knife in hand, facing the cow to be sacrificed. The moment was surreal—enacting an ancient tradition, a link in a chain stretching back countless generations.

As I plunged the dagger into the cow, emotions rushed through me—grief for my father, pride in fulfilling my duty, and a strange sense of connection to something larger than myself. The cow's life ebbed away, and I could almost feel the veil between physical and spiritual worlds thinning.

The rest of the ritual passed in a blur—preparing meat, sharing meals, prayers and invocations to the ancestors. I watched my extended family celebrate, not mourn. They came from far and wide, each with their own appeals to my father's returning spirit.

As the day ended, I felt exhausted yet relieved. I had performed the ritual, fed my family and community, and honoured my father. Yet, even as I basked in accomplishment, a small voice whispered that this was just the beginning of my journey, not its end.

2.4. The Feast of Ancestral Reverence: A Cultural Perspective on Abundance

The day of the ceremony arrived, and I had invited two of my friends, KG and AM, to join me for the weekend from Johannesburg. They came from different cultural backgrounds, one Tswana and the other Pedi. They arrived around 10 a.m., just in time for the first meal of braai meat, a tradition typically enjoyed by the men and boys as a reward for the hard work they perform including slaughtering the animals. They eagerly joined in, enjoying the feast.

At lunchtime, the main meal was served with even more meat, and again, we all indulged. However, by the evening, their initial enthusiasm had waned. They remarked on the sheer amount of meat being consumed, a stark contrast to their own cultural practices. By the next day, they barely touched their plates, overwhelmed by what they perceived as an excess of food.

Their reaction highlighted the resource-intensive nature of these Xhosa ceremonies. In a rural village, the expectation is to provide for the entire community, as everyone is welcome to partake in the feast. This open invitation, while embodying the spirit of generosity and communal unity, can lead to astronomical costs. The need to slaughter multiple animals, coupled with the expense of hosting numerous guests, places a significant financial burden on the family responsible for the ceremony. Meat is also not consumed alone so the food, desserts and alcohol must also be provided.

This experience with my friends underscored the cultural differences in perceptions of abundance and the practical realities of upholding traditional practices. It also served as a reminder of the economic challenges faced by many families in fulfilling their ancestral obligations.

3. Questioning and Conflict

As I delved deeper into our traditions, the subtle yet pervasive influence of Christianity on Xhosa spiritual practices became increasingly apparent. This realisation sparked a period of intense questioning and internal conflict, leading me to examine the very foundations of my cultural identity.

3.1. The Interplay of Traditions

The parallels between Xhosa traditions and Christianity were striking. Just as Christianity speaks of Jesus' death and resurrection, our Xhosa rituals describe the spirit leaving the home only to be welcomed back later. Both belief systems incorporate intermediaries between humans and the divine - ancestors for us, saints or Jesus for Christians.

However, a crucial difference emerged. In Xhosa tradition, my connection to Qamata (our creator) is facilitated through my family lineage. This necessitates nurturing these relationships through my conduct. Christianity, on the other hand, is authority-based; connection with God is achieved through Jesus, a figure with whom I, as a Xhosa man from Transkei, have no physical or genetic relation.

This realisation deepened my appreciation for our ancestral system. Without each of my predecessors, I wouldn't exist. Through them, I can trace a genetic link to my creator. My ancestors have a vested interest in my wellbeing because, for all their might in the spiritual realm, they can only act through the living. It's a mutually beneficial relationship - they need me as much as I need them.

3.2. Questioning Traditions

I found myself wondering: How much of what we practise is truly 'traditional'? How much has been shaped by centuries of interaction with Christian missionaries and colonisers? These questions were not merely academic; they struck at the heart of my identity and my understanding of our cultural heritage.

My ability to ask these questions was partly due to the circumstances of my upbringing. From the age of 13, I lived away from our village, pursuing formal education and employment. I returned only during school breaks and work vacations. This was my mother's arrangement; fearing for my safety after my father's death, and wanting to ensure I had a strong dependable male role model, she sent me to live with my uncle in another province. I will always admire her sacrifice and placing my interest first, because indeed, it takes a man to raise a man.

In this new environment, less dominated by Xhosa culture, I gained distance from the expectations of traditionalists. This allowed me the space to reflect on our customs and traditions, comparing them with those of other South African tribes. Had I remained in the village, the constant pressure to conform might have stifled my ability to question and critically examine these practices. My mother's wisdom and foresight in recognizing this have always filled me with awe and are just one of the many reasons I hold her in such high esteem.

3.3. Personal Doubts and Internal Struggles

As my understanding grew, so did my doubts. I questioned practices I had once accepted without thought. Why did we need to sacrifice animals to communicate with our ancestors? If our ancestors were truly omnipresent, why did we need to perform rituals at specific locations?

These doubts created a profound internal struggle. On one hand, I felt a deep connection to these practices - they were a link to my father, to my community, to centuries of Xhosa history. On the other hand, my rational mind grappled with aspects that seemed at odds with my evolving worldview.

Nights became battlegrounds of conflicting thoughts. Was I betraying my heritage by questioning these traditions? Or was critical thinking itself a form of respect, a way of engaging deeply with my culture rather than blindly accepting it?

Importantly, I knew that my parents had always encouraged questioning. They expected me to challenge traditions so that I could chart an appropriate course for my family based on sound reasoning rather than blind adherence to custom.

3.4. The Urban-Rural Divide

The conflict extended beyond the spiritual realm. As I built my career and moved to more urban areas, I felt the pull between modern life and traditional obligations. How could I balance the demands of my professional life with the time-consuming nature of these rituals? Was there a way to honour my ancestors that aligned with my contemporary lifestyle?

This urban-rural divide became a metaphor for the broader tensions I was experiencing. In the city, I was exposed to diverse perspectives and modern ways of thinking. Yet, each return to my rural roots brought me face to face with the expectations and traditions of my community. Navigating this divide became a central challenge in my journey.

3.5. Balancing Filial Duty with Personal Beliefs

Perhaps the most challenging aspect of this period was reconciling my sense of filial duty with my evolving personal beliefs. I knew that my father, had he lived, would have expected me to uphold these traditions. Yet, I couldn't shake the feeling that true respect for his memory meant being true to myself and my own understanding of the world.

I grappled with guilt. Each time I questioned a practice or considered not performing a ritual, I felt as if I was somehow betraying my father's memory. The weight of generations seemed to rest on my shoulders, and the fear of being the one to break the chain was almost paralysing.

3.6. Reframing Filial Duty

Yet, slowly, I began to reframe my understanding of filial duty. I reflected on my father's life - how he had adapted traditions to suit changing times, how he had encouraged me to think for myself. Would he really want me to blindly follow practices I didn't fully believe in?

I started to see that my duty to my father and my ancestors wasn't about unthinking adherence to tradition, but about living with integrity, making conscious choices, and carrying forward the best of our culture while allowing it to evolve.

This realisation was both liberating and terrifying. It meant that I had to take responsibility for shaping my own relationship with our traditions, with my ancestors, with my father's memory. It meant making choices that might not always align with community expectations.

3.7. The Path Forward

As I stood at this crossroads, I knew that the path forward wouldn't be easy. But I also knew that it was necessary - not just for me, but for future generations who would grapple with these same questions. In questioning and seeking understanding, I was not betraying my heritage, but engaging with it in the deepest possible way.

This period of questioning and conflict became a crucible for my personal growth. It forced me to confront the complexities of cultural identity in a rapidly changing world. I began to see that honouring my heritage didn't mean preserving it in amber, but rather allowing it to grow and adapt while retaining its core values.

As I moved forward, I carried with me a new understanding: that tradition and progress need not be at odds. By questioning, by seeking to understand, by adapting where necessary, I could honour my ancestors in a way that was authentic to my lived experience. This, I realised, was the true essence of filial duty - not blind obedience, but thoughtful engagement and evolution.

4. The Physical and the Spiritual

As my journey of questioning continued, I found myself returning to the fundamental Xhosa concept of burial: 'umhlaba emhlabeni, uthuli eluthulini' - earth to earth, dust to dust. This phrase, spoken at every funeral, began to take on new depths of meaning for me.

I pondered the symbolism inherent in this ritual. The act of returning the body to the earth is a powerful acknowledgment of the cycle of life and death. It speaks to the temporary nature of our physical existence and the eternal nature of our spiritual essence.

4.1. The Burden and Revelation of Grave Maintenance

One of my first burdens towards my father after he died was the maintenance of his grave, a physically demanding job that could mostly be done by me as the only male in the home. I had the primary responsibility of cleaning around my father's grave, shovelling all the weeds and making sure that the grave was always well-maintained and visible, as one would do when maintaining a home for the living. One day, visiting my father's grave, the full weight of this concept struck me. I watched as wind blew across the mound, carrying away small particles of soil. At that moment, I realised that my father's physical form was already becoming one with the earth, fulfilling the promise of 'umhlaba emhlabeni'.

This realisation led me to question: If we truly believe that the spirit is separate from the body, why do we place so much emphasis on the physical remains? Why does the location of a grave hold such significance if the spirit is free?

4.2. The Limitations of Confining Spirits to Physical Locations

As I grappled with these questions, I began to see the limitations of our traditional approach to ancestor veneration. We often acted as if our ancestors' spirits were confined to their graves or to specific locations where we performed rituals.

Having traced my roots from Central Africa in my previous book, I realised the utter shortsightedness of confining our ancestors to the graves that we could see. Considering to get to what is now the Eastern Cape, we left so many of our ancestors along the way. Did this now mean because we couldn't see their graves that the link is broken? This was illogical because the link to Qamata is continuous and unbroken from myself to my first parents, something that has been confirmed by science and biology. Cutting this link by only confining our ancestors to the graves we see would mean that it ends long before reaching Qamata. Within me there is also the Khoisan who mixed with some of my ancestors, but just as the Xhosa migrated to Transkei, the Khoisan had been nomadic for about 10,000 years with no fixed graves.

Until King Tshawe's reign and the final consolidation by King Hintsa, the Xhosa Kingdom did not exist but rather many tribes coexisted in the KZN area along with other descendants of Mnguni. This means that even within the last 400 years, we can't trace our graves for more than two or three generations. And what of those people that perished in the wild due to weather, nature, or animals and their remains were never found? Did this mean their descendants would have no link to Qamata? Many people even to modern day perished in violent wars and dangerous accidents with some men who worked in the mines dying underground with their bodies never to be found. Did these people no longer have a connection to Qamata?

In recent history alone there were many forced removals from places people called home through the bloody tribal wars in the KZN and Eastern Cape area right through to the bloody Mfecane and conquest by the colonisers, and forced removals during apartheid. Did these people no longer have a connection to Qamata? While slavery was not the norm in South Africa, there were people in the early days after colonisation who took up jobs which saw them venture into the sea never to be seen again when their ships perished before returning home. Did the descendants of these people no longer have a tie to their ancestors?

4.3. Rethinking the Connection Between Ancestors and Descendants

As I continued to reflect, I began to reconsider the nature of my connection to my ancestors, particularly my father. If his spirit wasn't confined to his grave or our old homestead, where was it? The answer, when it came to me, was simple and profound: within me.

I realised that my father - and all my ancestors - lived on through me in the most tangible way possible. Their genes shaped my physical form, their teachings influenced my thoughts and actions, their experiences were woven into the fabric of my life story.

This epiphany led me to a new understanding of ancestor veneration. Instead of looking outward to connect with my ancestors, I began to look inward. I started to see myself not just as an individual, but as the current embodiment of a long line of ancestors stretching back through time.

This shift in perspective was liberating. It meant I carried my ancestors with me wherever I went. I didn't need to be in a specific location or perform a particular ritual to connect with them. They were part of me, influencing my life in countless ways every day.

4.4. The Responsibility of Ancestral Legacy

At the same time, this realisation came with a profound sense of responsibility. If I was the living manifestation of my ancestors, then my actions and choices would shape how future generations connected with their ancestral heritage. It was up to me to live in a way that honoured this legacy while adapting it for the modern world.

As I stood at my father's crumbling gravesite, I no longer felt the anguish of abandonment or the weight of unfulfilled duty. Instead, I felt a deep sense of peace and connection. My father wasn't confined to this spot of earth - he was with me, part of me, guiding me as I navigated my own path through life.

4.5. Embracing the Infinite

This new understanding didn't negate the value of our traditional practices. Rather, it added a new dimension to them. Rituals and gravesites became not the sole points of connection with our ancestors, but powerful symbols and reminders of the continuous thread connecting past, present, and future.

In embracing this infinite connection, I found a deeper, more meaningful way to honour my ancestors. They were no longer bound by the constraints of physical locations. Instead, they lived on through the lives they touched, the stories they told, and the legacies they left behind.

My journey through questioning and understanding transformed my perspective on ancestral veneration. It allowed me to bridge the gap between tradition and modernity, finding a harmonious balance that honoured the past while embracing the present and future.

5. Freeing the Spirit, Embracing the Self

My journey of questioning led me to a profound realisation about the nature of spirits and our connection to them. I began to understand that by fixating on physical remains and specific locations, we were inadvertently limiting the very beings we sought to honour.

One day, as I stood before my father's weathered grave, a thought struck me with the force of revelation: My father had been freed from the constraints of physical existence. Why, then, was I insisting on binding his spirit to this patch of earth?

I remembered the words spoken at every Xhosa funeral: 'umhlaba emhlabeni, uthuli eluthulini'. We acknowledge that the body returns to the earth, but what of the spirit? Surely, it must be free to roam, to exist beyond the confines of space and time.

This realisation was both liberating and humbling. It meant that my father's spirit wasn't abandoned in our old home, nor was it trapped in the grave. It was free, unbounded, perhaps even omnipresent. The weight of guilt I had carried for years began to lift, replaced by a sense of wonder at the vastness of spiritual existence.

5.1. The Importance of Genetic and Spiritual Inheritance

As I embraced this new understanding, I began to see my connection to my ancestors, particularly my father, in a new light. I realised that the most tangible link between us wasn't a grave or a ritual site, but the very essence of who I am.

I started to pay attention to the subtle ways my father lived on through me - in my mannerisms, my values, even in my physical features. I saw how his teachings had shaped my worldview, how his experiences had influenced my choices.

This genetic and spiritual inheritance, I realised, was far more significant than any physical artefact. It was a living, breathing connection to my ancestors, one that evolved and grew with each passing day.

I remember looking at my hands one day and seeing my father's hands - strong, capable, marked by years of hard work. In that moment, I felt a surge of connection far more powerful than any I had experienced through traditional rituals. My father wasn't gone; he was here, a part of me, living on through my actions and choices.

5.2. Finding Ancestors Within Oneself

This shift in perspective led me to a revolutionary idea: the truest connection to our ancestors lies within ourselves. Instead of looking outward for spiritual connection, I began to look inward.

I started to see myself not just as an individual, but as a living embodiment of all my ancestors. Their strengths, their struggles, their wisdom - all of it was woven into the fabric of my being. This understanding brought with it a profound sense of responsibility and purpose.

I realised that honouring my ancestors wasn't just about performing rituals or maintaining gravesites. It was about living in a way that respected their legacy while adapting to the present and preparing for the future. It was about recognizing their influence in my life and using that awareness to guide my choices.

This inward focus didn't mean abandoning our traditions. Rather, it added depth and personal meaning to our practices. When I participated in rituals, I did so with a new understanding - not as someone beseeching distant spirits, but as someone acknowledging the ancestral wisdom within himself.

I began to see every choice, every action as a way of connecting with my ancestors. When I made decisions that aligned with the values my father had taught me, I felt his approval not as a distant spiritual force, but as an integral part of my own conscience.

This new perspective was transformative. It freed me from the geographical constraints of ancestor veneration. No matter where I went, no matter how far from my father's grave or our old homestead, I carried my ancestors with me. They were part of me, guiding me, supporting me.

Moreover, this understanding helped me bridge the gap between our traditional beliefs and the modern world. I could honour my ancestors not just through prescribed rituals, but through my daily life - through my work, my relationships, my contributions to society.

As I embraced this new way of connecting with my ancestors, I felt a sense of peace and purpose that had eluded me for years. The anxiety about neglecting my duties faded, replaced by a deep-seated confidence in my spiritual connection.

I realised that in freeing my father's spirit from the confines of the grave, I had also freed myself - from guilt, from rigid interpretations of tradition, and from the fear of losing connection with my roots. In finding my ancestors within myself, I had found a new way forward, one that honoured the past while embracing the future.

5.3. The Tip of the Iceberg: Ancestral Multitudes

To truly grasp the significance of our ancestral connections, consider the sheer number of ancestors required for one person to exist. Over a span of 400 years, roughly 16 generations, the number of direct ancestors exponentially increases. Each person has two parents, four grandparents, eight great-grandparents, etc. By the 16th generation, the number of ancestors reaches into the tens of thousands.

Extending this contemplation further, imagine a lineage tracing back to the birth of Jesus. Roughly two thousand years ago, this would encompass approximately 80 generations. The numbers become astronomical, involving millions upon millions of individuals. Each of these ancestors played a role as prerequisites in the chain of existence that culminated in the present generation.

What we see and know of our lineage, whether through physical graves or familial stories, represents only a tiny fraction of this vast ancestral network. If our connection to Qamata were based solely on physical connections, we would be so detached from our roots that the bond would seem almost non-existent.

Yet, the true connection is not physical but spiritual and genetic. Within us lies the essence of all those who came before, an unbroken thread that ties us to the beginning of humanity and beyond. This realisation underscores the profound depth of our heritage and the intricate web of life that sustains us.

In recognizing that what we see is just the tip of the iceberg, we gain a deeper appreciation for the vastness of our ancestry. This understanding liberates us from the constraints of physicality, allowing us to honour our ancestors in a more holistic and meaningful way. We are the product of countless lives, each one a vital link in the chain that leads to our existence. By looking within, we find a connection that transcends time and space, a connection that is both humbling and empowering.

6. Coming Full Circle

Years ago, I made a choice that diverged from the path many others take. Instead of leaving my mother and sisters behind in the Eastern Cape, content to visit them only during vacations or rituals, I decided to bring them with me. Given the Eastern Cape's status as one of the poorest and worst-performing provinces in the country, I knew their chances for a better life were slim if they remained there. The probability was high that I would return more often for funerals than for joyful visits.

As my sisters matured to adulthood, I recognized the potential for my role to expand beyond that of a brother and a provider for my family to that of a father figure. In our community, like many others, the absence of fathers is unfortunately common - a reality I understood deeply after losing my own father. This absence often leaves children in need of additional support and guidance.

Recognizing this, I naturally stepped into the father figure role, as my uncles did for my parent's grandchildren. While my mother and sisters provided invaluable care and nurturing, I realised I could offer additional resources and perspectives that complemented their efforts. It wasn't about comparing or diminishing their contributions, but rather about pooling our collective strengths as a family.

Given my circumstances, I was in a position to offer a stable home environment. It felt right to welcome my extended family into my home, providing a foundation from which they could grow and eventually build their own independent lives. This decision wasn't just about material provision, but about creating a supportive family unit where we could all contribute in our unique ways to raising the next generation.

By 2010, when my nephew Solo was born, it was mostly my mother and nephew who lived in my family home. My sisters had moved to Johannesburg to stay with me. Despite not having the means I had hoped for by 2016, my mother spent more time with us along with my nephew until I finally decided she could move up full-time.

With my family now in Johannesburg, I had little immediate reason to go to the Eastern Cape, and I was never eager to return. With no one staying there, my family home slowly started to wither, aided by criminals who were all too happy to help themselves to whatever was left behind. The first time I returned to my childhood home in over six years was in 2024.

6.1. Returning to the Eastern Cape

The main reason I went back to my childhood home was Tee, my partner. As if by fate, despite meeting Tee in Johannesburg, it turns out her father came from KwaSongwevu, not far from Fort Malan, where my father met my mother. My mother would tell me that for a brief time we actually stayed in the same village of Tee's family home, where her mother lays to rest and where I met her father. Had I not met Tee, who gave me a reason to go back because I wanted to meet her father and brothers and also take her to her family home, I most likely would still not have had a reason to go back.

After years of internal struggle and spiritual growth, thanks to Tee, I finally had enough reasons to return to my childhood home in the Eastern Cape. As I approached the familiar dirt road leading to our property, a mixture of anticipation and trepidation filled me. The sight that greeted me was far from the home I remembered. Crumbling walls stood as silent sentinels to the passage of time. The once-sturdy fence that had marked our territory now lay in disrepair, barely visible among the overgrown grass. Nature had begun to reclaim what was once ours.

As I stepped onto the property, memories flooded back. Here was the spot where my father had taught me carpentry, a skill that I have grown such that now I am not only able to build furniture items and perform renovations but frame a house. There was the tree that used to bear sweet peaches just before what was the small gate of the garden. And in the corner of what was once our yard, a mound of earth marked my father's grave.

I stood before this humble marker, emotions swirling within me. This was the moment I had both longed for and dreaded for years. How would I feel, seeing the physical manifestation of what I had left behind?

6.2. The Unexpected Catharsis

To my surprise, as I stood there taking in the scene, I didn't feel the crushing guilt or sorrow I had anticipated. Instead, a profound sense of peace washed over me. The anxiety that had gripped me for years began to dissolve.

I realised that what I was seeing was not abandonment or neglect, but the natural order of things. The crumbling walls, the overgrown grass, even the weathered mound of my father's grave - all of it spoke to the impermanence of the physical world.

In that moment, I truly understood the meaning of 'umhlaba emhlabeni, uthuli eluthulini'. My father had returned to earth, as we all must. The decaying structures around me were not a sign of failure, but a reminder of life's cycles.

I felt a weight lift from my shoulders. The guilt I had carried about leaving my father's remains behind melted away. I saw clearly that his spirit was not confined to this place, just as mine was not tied to the physical structures of my past.

6.3. Letting Go of Guilt and Finding Peace

As I stood there, surrounded by the remnants of my childhood home, I began to talk to my father. Not to his grave, but to his spirit that I now understood resided within me and around me.

I shared with him my journey, my struggles, and my new understanding. I thanked him for the lessons he had taught me, both in life and in death. I apologised for the years I had spent feeling guilty, realising now that this was never what he would have wanted for me.

As I spoke, I felt a sense of release. The bonds of obligation that had bound me to this place began to loosen. I realised that I had been carrying the weight of a misunderstood duty for far too long.

I saw that true respect for my father and our ancestors didn't lie in preserving physical remains or structures. It lay in carrying forward their wisdom, their values, and their spirit into the future.

I felt a profound sense of closure. I had come here seeking reconciliation with my past, and I had found it in the most unexpected way.

I took one last look at the mound that marked my father's grave. 'Thank you,' I whispered, not just to my father, but to this place that had shaped me, to the traditions that had guided me, and to the journey that had brought me to this moment of understanding.

As I walked away from the old homestead, I didn't feel like I was leaving my father behind. Instead, I felt him with me, within me, guiding me forward. I was not abandoning my past; I was carrying it with me into the future, transformed by understanding and acceptance.

7. Embracing Legacy and Duty

As I drove away from my childhood home, I felt a profound shift in my understanding of duty and legacy. The circle of life—birth, growth, death, and renewal—took on new meaning for me. I realised that my father's duty had been to provide for and guide his family, a role he fulfilled admirably during his too-short life. My duty, I now understood, was not to be bound by the past but to honour it by living fully in the present and preparing for the future. This knowledge I could now pass to my son, my nephews, and my niece, ensuring they never feel burdened or have to start where I did to understand this.

This new perspective transformed how I viewed my responsibilities. Instead of feeling burdened by the obligation to perform specific rituals or maintain a physical gravesite, I felt empowered to carry forward the essence of my father's teachings and our ancestral wisdom in my daily life.

I saw that the truest way to honour my father and our ancestors was to embody their best qualities, learn from their experiences, and build upon the foundation they had laid. This was a living, evolving form of respect—one that could adapt to changing times while maintaining the core values of our culture.

7.1. The Omnipresence of Ancestors

Perhaps the most profound shift in my thinking was the realisation that my ancestors, including my father, were not confined to any one place. They were everywhere—in the genes that shaped me, in the values I held, in the very air I breathed.

This understanding liberated me from the geographical constraints that had once defined my connection to my ancestors. I no longer felt that I needed to be in a specific location to commune with them. They were with me always, a part of me, guiding my steps and influencing my decisions.

I began to see signs of their presence in unexpected places—in the resilience I showed when facing challenges, in the wisdom that sometimes surprised me with its depth, in the instinctive actions that echoed the teachings of those who came before me.

This omnipresence of my ancestors became a source of strength and comfort. No matter where life took me, I carried my heritage with me. It was not a burden to bear but a wellspring of identity and guidance to draw upon.

7.2. Balancing Respect for Tradition with Personal Growth

With this new understanding came the challenge of finding balance—honouring our traditions while allowing for personal and cultural evolution. I realised that blind adherence to tradition without understanding its purpose could be as harmful as completely abandoning our cultural practices.

I began to approach our rituals and customs with a curious and critical mind, seeking to understand their deeper meanings and relevance to modern life. Some practices, I found, held timeless wisdom that was as applicable today as it was generations ago. Others, I realised, might need to evolve to remain meaningful in a changing world.

This balance became my new goal—to be a bridge between the past and the future, honouring the essence of our traditions while allowing them to grow and adapt. I saw that this approach not only enriched my own life but could also make our cultural heritage more accessible and meaningful to future generations.

In my professional life and personal relationships, I began to integrate aspects of our traditions in ways that felt authentic and relevant. I found that this approach often opened up meaningful dialogues about culture, identity, and values, allowing me to share the richness of our heritage in a way that others could appreciate and understand.

As I embraced this balanced approach, I felt a deep sense of authenticity and purpose. I was no longer torn between tradition and modernity, between duty to the past and aspirations for the future. Instead, I had found a way to honour both, creating a harmonious integration of my heritage and my lived experience.

7.3. A Journey of Transformation

This journey of understanding had transformed not just my relationship with my ancestors but my entire worldview. I saw now that our traditions, when understood deeply and practised mindfully, could be a source of strength and guidance in navigating the complexities of the modern world.

As I looked to the future, I felt a sense of excitement and responsibility. I had found my path—one that respected the past, embraced the present, and looked forward to the future. And in doing so, I had found a way to truly honour my father, my ancestors, and the rich cultural tapestry that had shaped me.

8. The Practical Logic of Ancestral Connections

The journey to understand our ancestors often focuses on spiritual connections, but there's a practical, tangible logic to maintaining these ties that becomes clear when we consider the evolution of language, culture, and identity over time. This chapter explores how our understanding of ancestral connections can be deepened by examining the practical aspects of cultural evolution and communication across generations.

8.1. The Evolution of Xhosa Identity

Xhosa identity is often defined through external markers such as language, clothing, and customs. However, these elements are not fixed; they evolve dramatically over time. This section will explore how our current conception of Xhosa identity might be unrecognisable to our ancestors from just a few centuries ago.

After my circumcision ceremony, a rite of passage marking my transition to manhood, I was expected to wear specific attire for about three months. However, as I returned to Pretoria to complete my studies, I removed this regalia before arriving. My decision was driven by a desire to integrate with the multicultural environment of Pretoria without imposing Xhosa standards of manhood. While logical, this choice caused me internal conflict for nearly two decades.

It wasn't until a conversation with my colleague and friend Bulelani, whom I met at work about 3-4 years ago, that I gained a new perspective. Bulelani, also Xhosa, helped me realise how recent many of our cultural markers, like specific clothing, truly are. This revelation freed me from my lingering guilt and highlighted the folly of attaching our identity too firmly to such changeable external elements.

8.2. Language as a Bridge and Barrier

Language, while a crucial part of cultural identity, also evolves rapidly. This section will explore how language changes can create barriers between generations and across centuries.

The incorporation of words from other languages into modern Xhosa, such as 'ifayidukhwe' from the Afrikaans 'vadoek' (dishcloth), demonstrates how our language adapts to new concepts and technologies. This evolution, while necessary, can create gaps in understanding between generations.

8.3. The Generational Communication Gap

Even within a span of a few generations, significant changes in language and culture can occur, creating communication challenges.

Personal Example: Both my grandmothers passed away in the 1960s and early '70s. If I could speak with them today, we would likely struggle to understand each other fully. My parents, particularly my mother who is still alive, act as a bridge between my grandparents' version of Xhosa and my own.

8.4. Time Travel Thought Experiment

If we could travel back in time, the differences between us and our ancestors would be striking. This section explores this concept through various time frames.

- **400 Years Ago:** A Xhosa person from this era would likely view us with the same awe and unfamiliarity as they did when first encountering Europeans or non-Bantu tribes. Our language and customs would be significantly different.

- **2000 Years Ago:** Our ancestors from this time might not even recognize us as part of their tribe. Our language, clothing, and customs would be so different that we'd be strangers to each other.

It's crucial to remember that until recently, the Xhosa were just one of many tribes in the Transkei area, not a unified kingdom. I am from the Bomvana tribe, which still exists today, as do descendants of the original Xhosa tribe. There were times when these tribes feuded and clashed over resources, even before external forces came into play.

This means that if I were to go back in time and identify myself as Xhosa to my Bomvana ancestors, they might perceive me as an enemy or stranger, depending on the relations between the tribes at that time. Similarly, before the mixing of Xhosa and Khoisan peoples, there were periods of conflict between these groups. If I were to encounter my Khoisan ancestors from a generation or two before this mixing, identifying as Xhosa could mark me as an enemy or outsider.

The further back we go, the more pronounced these differences become. At 20,000 years or more in the past, the cultural and linguistic differences would be extreme, potentially making any form of direct communication impossible.

8.5. The Continuous Chain of Understanding

This realisation highlights the crucial importance of maintaining a continuous link with each generation of our ancestors. Each generation serves as a bridge to the one before it, facilitating communication and understanding.

If our ancestors from thousands of years ago wanted to communicate with us, they would need to do so through each subsequent generation, as each one can explain the changes to the preceding one. This creates a chain of understanding that links us to our deepest roots.

8.6. Practical Implications for Ancestral Veneration

This perspective adds another layer of meaning to our cultural practices of ancestor veneration. It's not just about spiritual connection; it's about maintaining a chain of understanding that links us to our deepest roots. Each generation plays a crucial role in preserving and transmitting our evolving culture and identity.

8.7. Balancing Tradition and Evolution

Understanding this practical aspect of ancestral connections reinforces the importance of our traditions while also explaining why they must be allowed to evolve. It shows us that our identity is not fixed in external markers like clothing or even language, but in the continuous thread of understanding and adaptation passed down through generations.

This perspective allows us to honour our ancestors while also embracing change and growth. It encourages us to maintain strong connections with our immediate predecessors, as they are our direct link to our more distant past.

By recognizing the practical logic behind maintaining ancestral connections, we can approach our cultural practices with renewed appreciation and understanding. This perspective complements the spiritual aspects of ancestor veneration, providing a holistic view of why these connections are so crucial to our identity and cultural continuity. It reminds us that our role is not just to preserve, but to serve as a living bridge between past and future generations.

9. Lessons for the Future

I realised that for our traditions to remain relevant, they needed to evolve. While these traditions might add little to no value in directly communicating with our ancestors, they play a crucial role in bringing the family together, so that the living can support each other through hard times and celebrate the good times. We are a social people who, for the longest time, without private property, living a nomadic life, and enduring wars and battles that displaced my ancestors, believed our most valuable investment was in people rather than things. This belief held true then and still holds true now. Traditional activities and ceremonies facilitate those bonds, ensuring that family members know each other, even distant cousins and relations.

In performing my father's last ceremony, I met distant relatives I had never met before, and those I had only met seldomly. Seeing my extended family helped me learn more about myself. With a common ancestor, I could see how some traits I had inherited manifested in them, providing clues on how they might manifest in me. If it was something beneficial, I would amplify it; if it was something undesirable, I could modify it for the positive.

One example of this is my tenacity and determination, which has sometimes led my ancestors and relatives to act out in physical violence—a behaviour that was acceptable and even seen as a sign of courage at one time. However, while brute force might have worked for my ancestors, it is not as effective today. My challenge is to direct this potential for good. This is why I learned the value of physical work—to discharge the anger that drove them to act physically and channel it towards fueling my drive to change my family's future and challenge injustices, no matter how big the Goliath, through legal means that are relevant today.

9.1. Finding New Expressions for Core Values

This wasn't about discarding our heritage but about finding new ways to express its core values in a changing world. For instance, the tradition of slaughtering a cow for major ceremonies posed challenges in our urban life. Instead of abandoning the practice entirely, we've found ways to maintain its spirit. We come together as a family to share a meal, each contributing in some way— not with a cow, then with our time, resources, or skills. The essence of the tradition—coming together in unity and abundance—is maintained, even as its form changed.

I also saw opportunities to blend our traditions with modern practices. These adaptations ensured that our heritage remained a living, breathing part of our lives, guiding us and keeping us connected.

9.2. Finding Universal Truths in Cultural Practices

As I shared our traditions with others, including friends from different cultural backgrounds, I began to see the universal truths embedded in our practices. The respect for ancestors, for instance, wasn't unique to Xhosa culture. It reflected a human need to understand our roots and find guidance from those who came before us.

When I explained our traditions in terms of these universal principles, they resonated with people from all walks of life.

A colleague once told me how hearing about our ancestral practices had inspired him to delve deeper into his own family history, seeking wisdom from his grandparents' experiences. This universality became a bridge, allowing me to share the richness of our culture without imposing it on others. It opened up meaningful dialogues about values, identity, and the human experience that transcends racial and cultural boundaries.

I began to see how our Xhosa wisdom could contribute to broader conversations about community, respect for elders, and maintaining connections in an increasingly fragmented world. Our traditions, I realised, held lessons not just for us, but for society as a whole.

9.3. Becoming a Custodian of Heritage

As I looked to the future, I felt a sense of hope and purpose. The journey I had undertaken—from unquestioning acceptance, through doubt and conflict, to a new understanding—had equipped me to be a custodian of our heritage. Not as a gatekeeper rigidly enforcing old ways, but as a bridge builder, helping to carry the wisdom of the past into the future.

I saw my role now as not just preserving our traditions but helping them to grow and evolve. To remain living, breathing practices that could continue to guide and inspire, not just within our community, but beyond. The little boy who once stood bewildered at his father's funeral had grown into a man who could honour his ancestors by living fully, adapting wisely, and sharing generously. As I watch Solo and his generation engage with our heritage in new and meaningful ways, I feel a deep sense of satisfaction. The circle of life continues, and our ancestors' wisdom flows on, finding new expressions in each generation.

In this way, I realised, my father and all our ancestors lived on—not confined to graves or rituals, but alive in our actions, our values, and the lessons we passed on to the future. And in helping to ensure this continuity, I had found my own place in the great circle of our heritage.

10. Ancestral Reverence and the Golden Rule: A Universal Framework for Modern Ethics

In the face of not only South African but global moral decay and the shortcomings of traditional , religious and legal ethical frameworks, we find ourselves searching for a moral compass to guide us through the complexities of modern life. This chapter proposes a powerful yet often misunderstood source of ethical guidance: the integration of ancestral reverence with the universal principle of the Golden Rule. Far from being an antiquated belief system, this combination offers a universal, internalised moral framework that surpasses many contemporary ethical systems.

The concept presented here goes beyond the common perception of ancestral reverence as mere homage at gravesites or through ritualistic practices. Instead, it posits ancestors as omniscient moral guides, ever-present within us, working in harmony with the Golden Rule's principle of "Do unto others as you would have them do unto you." This redefined understanding has the potential to serve as a robust deterrent to immoral behaviour and a catalyst for ethical living, transcending cultural and religious boundaries.

10.1. The Biological and Spiritual Connection to Ancestors

At the core of this ethical framework lies an undeniable truth: we are the living embodiment of our ancestors. This biological reality, grounded in genetics, provides a tangible link to those who came before us. Every cell in our body carries the DNA passed down through generations, encompassing not just physical traits but the very essence of our being.

This biological connection is universal, making ancestral reverence a potentially unifying ethical base. Regardless of cultural background or personal philosophy, every human being has ancestors without whom they would not exist. This universality aligns perfectly with the Golden Rule, which is found across cultures and religions worldwide.

10.2. Beyond Physical Monuments: Redefining Ancestral Presence

Traditionally, many cultures have associated ancestral reverence with physical monuments, particularly graves. However, this grave-centric approach limits the moral potential of ancestral reverence. By confining ancestors to specific locations, we inadvertently restrict their influence on our daily lives.

To harness the full potential of ancestral reverence as a moral framework, we must recognize ancestors as omniscient observers, ever-present within us and around us. This shift in perspective creates a constant awareness of their presence, serving as a powerful moral compass that guides our actions at all times. This omnipresence aligns with the Golden Rule's emphasis on constant ethical consideration in our interactions with others.

10.3. Ancestral Reverence and the Golden Rule: An Internalised Moral Framework

The integration of ancestral reverence and the Golden Rule creates a robust, internalised moral framework. Both concepts derive their moral authority from within, making them resilient against external corrupting influences. This internalisation is what makes both ancestral reverence and the Golden Rule so powerful and universally applicable.

Key similarities include:

- Internal source of morality
- Universal applicability
- Empathy-based ethics
- Independence from external authority
- Proactive moral guidance

10.4. Advantages Over External Moral Systems

This integrated framework offers several advantages over external moral systems:

- **Universality:** Unlike specific religious or legal systems, ancestral reverence and the Golden Rule are accessible to all.

- **Constant accountability:** The omnipresence of ancestors and the self-reflective nature of the Golden Rule create a constant sense of moral accountability.

- **Personal relevance:** The framework connects personal behavior to a broader legacy, making ethical considerations more personally relevant.

- **Proactive approach:** Unlike reactive legal systems, this framework encourages ethical behaviour proactively.

10.5. Addressing Misconceptions and Abuses

It's crucial to address common misconceptions and abuses that can undermine the ethical potential of ancestral reverence. True ancestral reverence, combined with the Golden Rule, opposes any practices that harm individuals or communities, regardless of the intended purpose.

10.6. Application in the Modern World

This ethical framework adapts well to modern challenges while maintaining a connection to traditional wisdom. It can guide us in areas such as:

- Digital ethics
- Global citizenship
- Ethical consumerism

- Workplace ethics

10.7. Practical Application

When faced with an ethical decision, consider the following framework, which integrates the wisdom of ancestral reverence with the forward-looking principle of the best interests of the child:

- **The Golden Rule:** Begin by reflecting on how you would want to be treated in the given situation. This universal principle encourages empathy and consideration for others, fostering a sense of fairness and justice.

- **Intergenerational Legacy:** Reflect on how your ancestors would view your actions in light of the core Xhosa principle of protecting and preserving the family, especially the well-being and future of children (Ancestral Reverence). Would your choice honour the values and traditions passed down through generations? Would it contribute to a positive future for your children and their children?

- **Best Interests of the Child:** In line with the legal and ethical principle emphasised in "Beyond Redress: Prioritising the Child's Best Interests to Achieve Equality before the Law in South Africa" prioritise the well-being and development of children. Choose the path that best supports their physical, emotional, and psychological needs, ensuring their rights are protected and their future is secure.

- **Harmonizing Past, Present, and Future:** Integrate these considerations to make a decision that aligns with your values, respects your heritage, and safeguards the future. Remember that ethical choices are not made in isolation; they are part of a continuous thread connecting past, present, and future generations.

By embracing this holistic approach, you can navigate ethical dilemmas with wisdom and compassion, honouring your ancestors while ensuring a brighter future for generations to come.

10.8. A Path Forward in Ethical Living

The integration of ancestral reverence, the Golden Rule, and the best interests of the child offers a powerful, holistic approach to ethics that can guide us through the complexities of the modern world. This framework, rooted in internal reflection, cultural wisdom, and a deep concern for future generations, has the potential to foster a more empathetic, responsible, and ethically grounded society.

By recognizing the ancestors within us, applying the Golden Rule, and prioritising the well-being of children, we create a personal yet universally applicable moral compass. This approach, as explored in "Beyond Redress: Prioritising the Child's Best Interests to Achieve Equality before the Law in South Africa" combines the wisdom of our ancestors with the empathy-driven ethics of treating others as we wish to be treated, while also safeguarding the rights and needs of the most vulnerable members of our society. It offers a path forward in ethical living that honours our past, guides our present, and safeguards our future.

In the context of Xhosa tradition, this integrated framework emphasises the importance of family preservation and the continuity of ancestral values. By considering the impact of our actions on both our ancestors' legacy and our descendants' future, we ensure that our choices contribute to the well-being and flourishing of our families and communities. This approach aligns with the core principles of Xhosa spirituality, which values the interconnectedness of generations and the responsibility to uphold cultural traditions while adapting to the challenges of the modern world.

11. Conclusion

As I reflect on the journey that brought me here, from the confused eleven-year-old boy standing at his father's grave to the man I am today, I'm struck by the profound transformations I've undergone. This journey, born from the simple yet complex question of what to do with my father's remains, has led me through a labyrinth of cultural expectations, personal doubts, and ultimately, to a deeper understanding of myself and my heritage.

One of the primary reasons I embarked on this journey of research and reflection was for my son, as well as my nephews and nieces. For most of my life, I was burdened by the issue of what to do with my father's grave. I didn't want my son to carry the same weight I did. I wanted to provide answers and clarity for him, to free him from the cultural and emotional burdens that had weighed so heavily on me.

The path was not easy. I grappled with the weight of tradition, the pressure of societal expectations, and the internal conflict between honouring my past and embracing my present. There were moments of guilt, periods of questioning, and times when I felt torn between two worlds—the traditional Xhosa world of my ancestors and the modern world I inhabit.

But through this struggle, I've come to a place of peace and understanding that I never thought possible. I've learned that honouring our ancestors isn't about rigid adherence to practices we don't understand, nor is it about preserving their physical remains in a specific location. It's about carrying their wisdom forward, allowing their spirit to live on through our actions and choices.

I've discovered that my father—and all my ancestors—are not confined to a grave or a homestead. They are within me, part of my very being. They live in the values I hold, the decisions I make, and the legacy I'm creating. This realisation has freed me from the geographical and ritual constraints that once defined my connection to them.

Moreover, I've come to see our traditions not as immutable relics of the past, but as living, breathing practices that can and should evolve. The core values and wisdom they embody remain constant, but their expressions can change to remain relevant and meaningful in our changing world.

This journey has also shown me the universal truths embedded in our cultural practices. The respect for those who came before us, the importance of understanding our roots, the need for guidance from accumulated wisdom—these are human needs that transcend cultural boundaries. In sharing our traditions, I've found connections with people from all walks of life, bridging divides and fostering understanding.

As I look to the future, I see my role not just as a preserver of tradition, but as a bridge builder. I have the responsibility and the privilege of helping to carry the wisdom of our ancestors forward, adapting it for new generations and sharing it with the wider world. In doing so, I honour my father and all those who came before me in the truest sense.

This journey has also profoundly influenced my thoughts about my own death and burial. From a young age, I resolved that when I die, I don't want to be a burden to my son or tie him down to a physical location. Initially, I considered cremation, but I've come to question even that, as it requires energy to release the energy left in my remains. In truth, I would prefer for my remains to be abandoned in the wild, allowing animals to feed on them, repaying my debt to nature, and leaving no trace of a monument to bind my son.

If I am to be buried, I want it done in a place where, like my father's grave, it will naturally fade away until it becomes one with the earth. No tombstones, no memorable monuments. There should be no fuss, no financial burden on my family. The cheapest, most biodegradable casket will do—preferably made of pine, as it's natural and affordable. My family may have lost my physical presence, but they must never bind themselves to a gravesite or monument, nor burden themselves with unnecessary costs.

To those who may be on a similar journey, grappling with questions of tradition, duty, and identity, I offer this: Don't be afraid to question, to doubt, to seek understanding. Our traditions are strong enough to withstand scrutiny. In fact, it's through this process of questioning and reinterpretation that they remain alive and relevant. Remember that honouring your ancestors isn't about maintaining a physical location or performing rituals without understanding. It's about carrying their spirit forward, embodying their wisdom in your life, and building upon the foundation they laid. Your ancestors live on through you—in your DNA, your values, your actions. You are their living legacy.

And to my son, nephews, and nieces, for whom this journey was primarily undertaken: May you find in these pages the answers and understanding I sought for so long. May you be free from the burdens I carried, able to honour our ancestors without being bound by outdated practices or physical monuments. Your connection to our heritage is within you, not in any grave or ritual. Carry it forward, adapt it, and make it meaningful for your own lives and times.

As I close this chapter of my life, I do so not with a sense of finality, but with an openness to continued growth and understanding. The journey doesn't end here. Our traditions, like life itself, are ever-evolving. And in that evolution, in the passing of wisdom from one generation to the next, in the constant reinterpretation and renewal of our heritage, our ancestors truly live on.

Umhlaba emhlabeni, uthuli eluthulini—earth to earth, dust to dust. But the spirit? The spirit is free, boundless, eternal. It lives in us, through us, and beyond us. And in understanding this, I have found my peace, my purpose, and my place in the great circle of life. May you, too, find your peace and your place, unburdened by the physical trappings of death, free to honour our ancestors in ways that are meaningful and relevant to your lives.

Appendices

Glossary of Key Terms

- **Ancestors:** In Xhosa culture, ancestors are revered spirits of deceased family members who are believed to guide and protect the living.

- **Mfecane:** A period of widespread chaos and warfare in southern Africa during the 19th century.

- **Qamata:** The supreme being or creator in Xhosa spirituality.

- **Rondavel:** A traditional round hut with a conical thatched roof, common in Southern Africa.

- **Umhlaba emhlabeni, uthuli eluthulini:** A Xhosa phrase meaning "earth to earth, dust to dust," often spoken at funerals.

- **Xhosa:** A Bantu ethnic group predominantly found in South Africa, known for their rich cultural traditions and language.

- **Salatiso:** A Xhosa name meaning "show us the way," given to the author by his father.

- **Mlandeli:** A Xhosa name meaning "to follow," given to the author's father by his grandfather.

- **Sazisi:** The author's son's name, with one of the meanings consistent with the author's name hence used in the place of Contents.

Bibliography

- Theal, George McCall. *Kaffir (Xhosa) Folk-Lore*. Swan Sonnenschein & Co., 1886.

- Mdeni, Salatiso Lonwabo. *Getting to know yourself as a South African, Unravelling Xhosa History: A Journey from Central Africa to South Africa*. 2024.

- Mdeni, Salatiso Lonwabo. *The Homeschooling Father, How and Why I got started*. 2023.

- Mdeni, Salatiso Lonwabo. Beyond Redress: Prioritising the Child's Best Interests to Achieve Equality before the Law in South Africa. 2024

- Krog, Antjie. *Country of My Skull*. Random House, 1998.

- Peires, Jeffrey B. *The Dead Will Arise*. Ravan Press, 1989.

- Mqhayi, Samuel Edward Krune. *Ityala Lamawele*. Lovedale Press, 1914.

- Jordan, A. C. *Ingqumbo Yeminyanya*. Oxford University Press, 1940.

- Hunter, Monica. *Reaction to Conquest*. Oxford University Press, 1936.

- Wilson, Monica, and Leonard Thompson (eds.). *The Oxford History of South Africa*. Oxford University Press, 1969.

- Opland, Jeff. *Xhosa Oral Poetry*. Cambridge University Press, 1983.

- Hodgson, Janet. *The God of the Xhosa*. Oxford University Press, 1982.

Additional Resources

- Online resources for Xhosa history and culture
- Xhosa language learning materials
- Contemporary Xhosa writers and thinkers
- Organisations working to preserve and promote Xhosa culture

Author's Note on Further Research

This book is a personal journey through Xhosa tradition and spirituality, but it is by no means exhaustive. I encourage readers to continue exploring these topics, to question, and to seek understanding. While the bibliography and additional resources provided here can serve as starting points, I urge you to look beyond formal sources of knowledge.

To put into perspective how recent formal education systems are in human history, let's imagine the entire span of human existence compressed into a single year:

If January 1st represents the emergence of early humans about 300,000 years ago, formal schooling as we know it today wouldn't appear until December 31st at around 11:59 PM. The vast majority of human knowledge, wisdom, and cultural transmission occurred without formal educational institutions for 364 days and 23 hours of our metaphorical year.

This stark comparison highlights the immense value of informal knowledge and unarticulated wisdom that has guided our species for millennia. For those interested in delving deeper into their own language and culture, I strongly recommend starting first within, then your own parents and larger family. This is far more important because most of our wisdom is not written down and is communicated orally. Even the best attempts at recording it miss many nuances.

Don't underestimate the value of lived experience, personal stories and oral histories from elders in your community. These can provide invaluable insights that you won't find in any textbook. While cultural institutions, universities with African Studies programs, and community organisations can offer valuable resources, remember that formal systems are incredibly recent compared to the deep well of wisdom within our families and communities.

It's crucial to recognize that every individual, regardless of their level of formal education, possesses priceless knowledge and wisdom. In our current times, especially given the challenges facing South Africa in 2024, we must not overlook the importance of diverse perspectives and traditional knowledge systems.

While I have gained much knowledge through formal systems, I have also learned their shortcomings, as articulated in my book, The Homeschooling Father. Many people look down on informal knowledge and unarticulated wisdom due to pressure to conform and the perception that these informal systems are old and antiquated. This is far from the truth, especially since we have seen the failures brought about by directing the masses towards formal systems, resulting in the unfortunate state that South Africa is in today.

Remember, our understanding of culture and tradition is always evolving. I invite you to contribute to this ongoing dialogue, to share your own experiences and insights, and to help shape the future of our cultural heritage. By valuing both formal and informal knowledge, by respecting the wisdom of our elders alongside academic research, we can work towards restoring power to individuals and families, and create a more holistic understanding of our rich cultural legacy.

As we delve into Xhosa culture, history, and personal reflections, remember that this book is not just about looking back, but about forging ahead. It's about recognizing the value in both formal and informal knowledge, respecting the wisdom of our elders while embracing the potential for growth and change.

This is our story - my father's, mine, my son's, and by extension, the story of my whole family and countless others navigating the complex interplay of tradition and progress. May it inspire reflection, dialogue, and a deeper appreciation for the generations that shape us.

Ultimately, this book stands as a tribute to my father and a message to my son, bridging the wisdom of the past with the promise of the future.

www.ingramcontent.com/pod-product-compliance
Lightning Source LLC
Chambersburg PA
CBHW021809150726
47989CB00004B/1845